BETWEEN**STONE** AND**FLESH**

POETRY & CREATIVE PROSE WINNERS OF
LAKE SUPERIOR WRITERS' CONTEST 2002

Lake Superior Writers
2002
Duluth, MN

Between Stone and Flesh is the anthology of winning manuscripts from Lake Superior Writers' Contest 2001/2002, which accepted entries from the Lake Superior region on "The Nature of Love, The Love of Nature." This year's jurors were: poetry, Robert Hedin; creative prose, Carol Bly. Special thanks to our preliminary readers: Connie Wanek and Konnie LeMay.

Lake Superior Writers' Contest 2001/2002 is an activity of Lake Superior Writers, a non-profit writing organization based in Duluth, MN. To learn more about our organization and activities, write to: Lake Superior Writers, P.O. Box 3025, Duluth, Minnesota 55803.

Between Stone and Flesh is published by Lake Superior Writers, Post Office Box 3025, Duluth, Minnesota 55803.

Cover art & design by Lisa McKhann, Project Lulu.

Edited by Lisa McKhann, Jim Perlman, and Mara Kirk Hart.

The Lake Superior Writers' Contest 2001/2002 gratefully acknowledges the following contributors: The College of St. Scholastica–English Department; Duluth Public Library; Holy Cow! Press; Minnesota Power; Northern Lights Books & Gifts; University of Minnesota Duluth–Tweed Museum and Library; and the University of Wisconsin Superior–Department of Language and Literature.

This activity is made possible in part by a grant from the Arrowhead Regional Arts Council through an appropriation from the Minnesota State Legislature.

CONTENTS

CREATIVE PROSE

POETRY

JAN CHRONISTER

STEEL HEARTS

She wears steel hearts
hanging from her ears,
glistening like the hood
of her daughter's gray car
buckled around a pole.

Steely like
dentist's tools touching teeth,
a cold mailbox
holding bills.

Love is not red and soft
and chocolate,
it is malachite and salt and ice,
frozen waves of Superior
on the freighter deck
her father went down on,
broken hull
laying stiff in dark depths.

Love is wet hands on
aluminum doors at
twenty below,
digging out tires
embedded in snow
with nothing but a cardboard box.

A bell tolls,
A lock turns.
She hammers an unforgiving nail
and steels her heart.

AFTER LOVE

I feel like a plowed field,
batter that has been beaten
the required two hundred strokes,
a tree with a hollow
at its base.

Do you feel like a plowblade,
spoon,
or raccoon?

I feel longer,
do you feel shorter?

AMNICON CONFESSION

Seven o'clock,
coffee in hand,
the pilgrimage begins.

Lacy rivers race under the road.
I want to worship at old stone bridges,
baptized by spray.

Pine and birch fly by,
flat and senseless.
Speed and glass
obscure the odor
of gold needles underfoot-
incense of a shrine
I have no time to visit.

White of an eagle
catches my eye,
but I have to watch the road now.
I'm coming down to the Amnicon,
last bridge before town.

Two local women died here,
head on
daylight
road dry.
Maybe they were looking
at the sky.

ERIK GADZINSKI

ASHMUN

It doesn't look like much,
weedy and trashed,
a rutted dirt track.

Nobody goes there,
only the wind hushes,
a gull wheels and calls.

Sometimes a walker passes
striding somewhere
and does not notice.

But here
the sky is bluest,
the sun highest at noon.

Here in the litter of the world's neglect,
among cast-off wrappers,
and the glitter of broken glass,

under a spare and plaintive tree,
the grass is matted
where we lay.

JIIGIBIIK

I have been there.
I have seen it.
A blue water
says a name
over and over.

Two arms
of green pines
and white birch
reach out to hold
a pearl eternity.

And she sits
on a blanket.
Her brown eyes
and pure lips
the breeze praises.

I can prove it,
for when I woke
in the gray day
a sand-gold strand
of hair she left me.

WINTER SOLSTICE

Now the snow
ticking the gray quiet
of bare boughs,
whiteness imperceptibly
forgetting what we knew:
fallen leaves, a footprint
frozen in mud.

The tiny crystal
that burns and weeps my cheek
is that vast geometry
of worlds and suns
spinning the elegant, inevitable
idiocy of ellipse
from perigee to apogee,

so that this is how it must be:
not truth, desire, philosophy,
but the random reason
of bodies in a motion
not their own, thrown
by what spark
of a volatile complacency

into this all-day twilight,
the steady, blank accumulation,
the cramp of cold, the golden
glow from warm windows
as I turn away down a long,
lone road in a wordless wood
to where it bends and vanishes.

And then? Back again?
Beyond what we imagine,
by a senseless, circular calculation,
although nothing's certain,
where deep dreams melt, a new
and strange green grass
may flame through dead ribs.

PATRICIA KIRKPATRICK

LETTER TO THE UNFINISHED

The night we ate licorice
was like being young again.
No one had died, no one had carried
a bell jar of vodka
each morning to the hospital,
snuck it into a bag
with clean socks and tablets.
No one had crossed
anyone off anyone's list.
We still went over the bridges
singing.
Then we grew up.

But I remember promises
and arrivals on platforms
as trains pulled into the station.
Highstrung and handsome,
we were the children of sisters
in distant cities
and we loved each other.
Holidays they lined up all the cousins
as if we were horses:
this one is golden,
this one better learn to stand straight,
this one has a mouth on her.
I walked down the hall after dinner,
thrilled as I entered the room
of burning candelabras,
to bring the fathers their leaded
glasses of cognac.
Kissing one man as I set amber
in his hand, smiling

at the other, flirting
a little, yes
I wanted them to adore me.

What you wanted
and what you got in that house
we never spoke of.
Years before, your father
pushed a plush towel
through my legs
then let me stand on his shoes
the next night as we danced in circles.
What would I have told you?
You were always smiling, a bronze boy with cheeks
as smooth as fruitwood.
No one had lost their teeth yet,
watched a brother shoot heroin,
gone AWOL from rehab, fled
murderous debt.
No one had forbidden
one cousin to speak to the other.
For years, I had nothing
but stories of what happened to you.

Reunited by a death, I knew
we shouldn't kiss on the lips
but I wanted to touch you.
The house was different with a bed
and commode in the drawing room.
Still you set the candy in celadon cups.
You lit candles and took me
to see lacquer, statues, and portraits.
Your long-fingered hands
opened drawers
and took out my picture.
You wanted to praise me.
I wanted to save you.

I didn't expect a man the height of your father.
The licorice sticks stood up
straight as pencils
we could write the stories with.
 Don't go back I whispered.
I have unfinished business
you answered.
I bit into the licorice, sucking
to put the resinous proof on my mouth.
Like you,
I have been touched.
I have taken part here.
Then like a mare being led from the paddock,
I paused,
wanting to choose my last run in this house.

for *CJH*

LETTER TO MY NAMESAKE

Once I wanted to do whatever you did,
starting with language,
speak those key words and phrases
handwritten on notecards in English and French
you gave me,
the eight year younger cousin who was named for you.

When I'm handed the phone
to speak my condolences
the first time we've spoken in 25 years
I hear your immaculate diction
describe the blue sky and clouds
you see swirled with your mother's spirit.

Your brothers talked you out of coming for her funeral
just as your mother insisted they keep you
from coming to visit the last days of her life.
You agreed to stay in California
if they would let you speak to
everyone here.

I want to know the diagnosis
a sister asks after the service.
When your son answers
violent rages and abandonment issues
he surrenders the truth we've suspected:

when the eyebrow of your listener rises,
when the face of the mountain
flares and clatters with traffic, when
coffee is radioactive,

you flee in the night
and are homeless.

Clouds move along, pale and fragrant as oolong.
No code a brain throws

makes a mind fade entirely.
You still speak Chinese and Russian,
walk with conjugated pockets
of French verbs and madness
pinned to your dress.
I saw you graduate from high school,
brilliant valedictorian
with sixteen other girls wearing white dresses,
your hair crowned with gentians.
When did you drift, anguished, into blazes
and take glinting blades in your hands?

The bar where you blurted
he balled me and so did his sons
shook a cocktail of planets
revolving with halogen
the last time I saw you.

We lived briefly once in the same city.
Relatives told me not to give you my address
when broke and addicted,
you called,
and I never did.
Now you fear being followed, give no one
your whereabouts.
Enraged at your mother and the neighboring world
who left you in an orphanage once for a year,
which leaves you such luminous wandering now
under streetlamps of rapture and trash—
how many city blocks in a night?

Un, deux, trois. The numbers you taught me
come over the face of the mountain
unsummoned. These are the cards we drew.
I write the words down as you did once for me.
Whatever I write has your name on it.

KATE KYSAR

THE PREGNANT WIFE EATS DIRT

It is gray everywhere: coal soot
on the eaves, rain changes to sleet
changes to dirty white snow. We
have nothing to eat but potatoes,
turnips, and bread. I crave
green: braised kale, spinach,
even shredded cabbage.
The sky is pregnant too—full
of round clouds scudding the sky.
I barter the ring for a cabbage,
make soup, but it doesn't satisfy.

One night, when they are all asleep,
I touch the tip of my tongue to a sliver of coal,
but it is gritty, dusty, and black.
The next day, the children napping,
I take a tablespoon into the garden,
dig under the icy layer of snow to the gray clay dirt
beside the fence. I put the spoon to my mouth.
It tastes of aluminum, feces, and clay pots.
I put my spoon in again, lift it to my lips,
then hear my neighbor splashing her wash water
out the door. I stand, smooth my apron,
slipping the spoon inside the pocket,
wanting the sky to darken, the moon
to open up and swallow me, feed me
rocks and gold, minerals and diamonds,
all the hardness in the world
to make this baby grow soft.

POEM FOR DARK LAKE

1
The old Indian man rose from the lake
and took my almost sleeping hand.
I too was Anishinaabe. We rose into the sky
above the misty, humid clouds,
into whiteness. There, his magnified hand
holding pine seeds, he said,
"Sprinkle these around the lake."
The seeds poured from his hand to mine.
I scatter them around the edges of the lake.
The dream ends.

2
I swim out
into the cool water,
my swimsuit cumbersome,
keeping me from joining the fish of the shallows,
the bubbles of oxygen that rise to meet my each step on shore.

I swim out
past the calm water
into the rippled current to the ominous peninsula
haunted by lilypads and broken floating wood.
I pause. Three pine trees
on Lee and Dolly's land sprout straight and tall
from the white birch forest.
They are the pine trees I planted in my dream.

3
The woman across the lake
makes sweat lodges for her children.
They learn ceremonies of tobacco and thanks.
She is a fierce wolf mother
and dislikes my city smells.

I show her the peonies,
tell her of my dream. She nods.
I am awake. The sky sprinkles seeds of rain on us.

BODIES OF WATER

Elsie wrote
on the newspaper lining
her sewing cupboard
mothers are the ocean
their children swim in.
The baby inside me burps, flips,
confirming her truth. The mother
is the ocean and the boat, the rubber raft
and the assailing storm, the water their bodies float in.

≈

Marlon's cells
are rebelling, sewing nebulous, flesh
into shadowy, unconfirmed masses.
He awaits the tests as these cells
flourish at night in the dark,
sapping his energy, using his fat,
growing these strange fruits.

≈

The baby converts my dinner
into flesh, into eyes and nose,
brain cells and bone. It takes my energy
plus apple juice to make blood.
It takes the car song of its brother
and makes movement, a leg or hand
hitting the sides of its uterine walls
to the internal waves of sound.

≈

Marlon,
I am eating a pumpkin pie for you tonight.
I am eating Caribbean rice. I am drinking whole milk
and dreaming of breakfast with toast and butter.
I am converting this food into energy into mass into
cells into baby. I wish I could give you some.

≈

What is it like to live in a home of water,
to breathe and drink the fluid of mother ocean,
buoyant and salty and clear?
Is it the purest of sensations?
I lay curled in the bathtub at night,
the lights turned low, mineral salts in the water,
the womb within the womb,
a mother becoming an ocean.

≈

My neighbor tells me stories of Elsie:
Elsie plants a Haralson apple tree at age 98;
Elsie's scraps of scribbled sewing paper;
the night she sits on her porch during a storm,
a huge elm crashes down, its leaves
brushing her screen windows, her roof.
I always wanted to see a tree falling,
she said calmly, in awe, in wonder.
Perhaps my time had not come.

≈

Marlon is pale and accepting;
he has cleared his heart to calm.
Remission: he stitches words into paper with paint.
Perhaps my time has not come.
The ocean inside him rises, cleansing water
of peace. He wakes from the dream,
sips a glass of water, and breathes.

DIANE SHER LUTOVICH

SO HARD TO HOLD ON

Hiking with my daughter
along the California coast
we carry our lunch–golden apricots,
oranges, whole-grain bread,
a bottle of cold water.

At the crest, the Pacific,
flat and blue rolls out at our feet

In the distance, two deer,
a bobcat moving suspiciously
across the slope

Years back, our cat, still unformed,
dropped five kittens under the bed
rolled on her back, bared her nipples.

After five weeks, sucked dry,
we sent Carmen away, long enough
for her milk to dry up, her babies
to new homes.

Back, she wandered
a day or two, seemed to settle,
chewed nipples, distended belly, quiet.

≈

Near the end of the trail we talk
of big things–her future

she'll stay home with her children

I don't argue.
I have no news.

but the sea, the Pacific,

the sun, fog
the certainty of my own
insignificance.

On the way to the car, we pass ponds–
she remembers catching tadpoles
trying to turn them to frogs,
the one that made it as far as its hind legs.

I remember my mother splitting open a walleye,
its orange globs of eggs slipping
Out of the belly
through her hands,
onto the floor.

ALL IS GOLD

When runners carrying gold to free their king,
Atahualpa, heard he'd been strangled,
they buried the gold beneath their feet.

Paddling this astonishing
Pacific-bound stream, I'm caught
by the Sun shedding,
sprinkling golden discs
merging, separating,
finally binding themselves
into one blinding path
leading up and back.

No wonder Egyptians, Incans
all people living close
to the natural world craved gold
as if cast off by the sun,
with one blaze illuminating the wearer,
mirroring its sources. Of course
they covered themselves in death with
the same sacred sun-reflecting surface.

This morning I could have
paddled or drowned in that path
dragged across the water by the sun
trolling for people like me
who want to melt into its power
but too frightened
to approach its center, afraid
of burning their eyes,
never finding home again.

WHAT THE BODY KNOWS

Hiking up the canyon
in the Prima Vera Wilderness,
feet balance, thighs thrust,
the body a part of and separate from

My mind wanders
to lunch, last evening's talk,
eyes register hunks of worked obsidian,
blistering blue lady slippers, *violete de monte*

I leave feet struggling for foothold,
to make their way without
guidance—resting on plateaus, digging into
slippery scree, stepping away from
treacherous spikes of *agave tequilana*

Sweat slides down cheeks,
into creases of elbows, that fine crevasse
between thigh and pelvis; under breasts

Spiraling back to base,
I think of these body parts
turning in love, how there, too,
head sneaks off to its own vistas,
memories, caches of desire

as if we started a hike up the arroyo together
and returned, damp, joyous, sated.

MARK MAIRE

LETTER

The letter you were intending to write
Arrived yesterday. I charted its course
By air over a snow-covered landscape
Of dark clotted pines and crystalline lakes.
It said nothing had changed—made no mention
Of disunion, of gaping holes in time.

When the snow melts in this city of cliffs,
Someone will find it, wedged between two rocks:
Ink blurred, passion spent, addressee unknown.
It never reached me at my blue window,
My chink of lake from the attic's east end:
High seas, safe harbors, and no word from you.

PORTAL

In memory of C.A.O.
(1949-1998)

Largesse is piled on largesse as June peaks
In a garden hose mist of fine green rain.
It glistens in black beads on fresh asphalt,
Makes flecks on the windows of waiting cars,
Collects on heaping peony blossoms.

Strange then to think of so many dark things:
Insects in their underground catacombs,
The smell of rotting wood in heavy air,
Bees moored in their hexagonal chambers,
The pine woods enveloped in late darkness.

Heat rising, lightning is a confluence
Up from the earth, not a bolt from above.
I think of windows pummelled by hail,
Absorbing the blows that suddenly stop:
As when the light in an upstairs window

Went out as I drove through Siren at dusk:
A consciousness snuffed out, a sudden death–
First the violent pelting, then nothing
But an unexpected flush of cold air:
Such a faint blue breath, so light on the skin.

AFTER THE ICE STORM

The cashier at Menard's sported a hank
Of hair the exact color and texture
Of pink insulation material,
But her eyes revealed a docile spirit
Who counts herself out at too young an age.
I drove home with my new hatchet and saw
Beside a ghostly hillside of sheer rock
And pines that writhed upward in peaks and whorls.

There were so many severed limbs thrown down!
The rains that followed washed so much away.
The old moon held the new moon, both cut off.
Send me the angel that roams this hillside:
The wild one with a fugitive heart,
Who delicately mends all that's severed,
And rebuilds the landmarks without which we are lost.

LISA MCKHANN

JAZZED

Jazz appears in a blue sedan.
When I look up, he's there
beyond the shoppers and gawkers,
street hawkers and God talkers.
When I look up, jazz appears
in a dark blue sedan.
"What's your name, dear?" he asks,
smoothest sax,
he unpacks his bags,
instruments shapely tropical fruits,
sweet soulfulness of mango tango,
my one-man band.
Play it.

THE ROWER

slips by, a zipper
through evening's
silk gown.

Light splits
golden threads
of sequins
in his wake.

Dark whispers
his urging
warm breath
upon my neck.

I am, in one stroke,
unzipped, undone,
my skin, the water
his craft will ply.

A SIMPLE THING

In Mother's arms
I rest
breasts and bellies pressed close
still until our hearts meet
our breaths even
her pulse ours
our wordless yes
each other's only
presence so full
no room exists
beyond the neat fit
our bodies make
in this lingering

MARY KAY RUMMEL

HARTLAND POINT

Who are those that fly

like cloud

enter into rock

a clarity in

become salt

become thunder

stricken

waterfall in one ear

surf in the other

oil of gladness
        mantle of praise

spirit riding
      the body

knocked to the ground
     by wanting

*After listening
to Beethoven's
Ninth I step
into city light*

*the sideways
slant*

in the brain

a sudden seeing

it's like that

inside

outside

the same

*I have been
wanting (this)
lightning*

*a transformation
what is*

happy with campion   *far*
            rock   *to be*
            tidepool clamour
            feasts   feasts   *near*

all senses like tentacles   *closer than*
                                         I thought

THIS IS HOW SHE WILL NOT

talk about loss anymore
that shadow that makes leaves shine.
She will go to Jackson Square, watch women
parade in pastel dresses and filmy hats
drink chicory coffee in the garden
while a mime dressed as an angel
lifts announcing arms
and the psychics set up stalls
she will not enter.

In Vermont a man paints his porch
and sings as he paints
old melodies of love and   (   )
(she will not say it)
follow her.
I've hungered for your touch
he sings into the day that is fine
a long lonely time he moans
to clouds hiding the highest peaks.

At home she will not write of (   )
All night the window open
to the two sounds of the lake.
Church bells scour deserted streets
The lighthouse blinks on its rock.

Even in October she will not
when the solidity of things
bay   barge
consonants of truck on bridge
call back the ones she has   (   )
when Superior churns them up, ragged
saying *yes, you know us we're yours*
then swallows them again
while gulls cry *mine, mine, mine.*

so much   (   )
among us.

CAIRNS

1

The Loch is slate air, peat smoke and mist.
We find in the sodden field among cows and sheep
the stone age graves flanked by standing stones
No one really knows who the Picts were
or what's in these graves appeasing their gods.

2

I set up tripod and the camera
comforted by its whir and story myself back.
At first only the sound of sheep bells distracts
a bleat, a moo, the feeling of being among

until a couple and their two children
arrive, talking as they find ancient
doorways, stone beds, barn, byre.

Both scientists, they know the whys
of stone. What I hear is hidden between.
The parents' eyes are flint.

3

The stones like those works of modern art
white paintings on white walls
tell only different ways of seeing
say all is relationship, everything counts
in blank fields, hovering on the edge of sense.
Possibilities make their own light,
scraps of touch, touching
behind them, a hand quavers.

4

Echoes spin round me, wind-riven.
When you sink into such a place death could
come upon you the way it did the old Scots woman
who was resting on a rock in her field.

Death made her part of the field
of the run-on sentence of snow,
the afterthought whispers of flake.

5
Underneath my life is a life
I have chosen not to live

Adumbratio on water, in air

Between stone and flesh

between fragment and completion

between trace and memory

distance so great it is not

JASON SPLICHAL

AFTER GEORGE HOLZ'S 1996 GELATIN SILVER PRINT: WOMAN, GARDEN OF AGAVE, TEQUILA, MEXICO

The sharp
Flat
Rays of agave shine upward
On her round
Lean legs and arms
Scissored
In a gentle gate
Their insides
A tawny cream
Joined to a midriff
Shaded
By firm breasts
Bulging to perfect points
Under an insatiable sun
Thick hair
Trickles like night
Down the furrows
Straddling her spine

Like all
Our familiar paramours
Her face is a soft shadow
An impossible parallax
Each of her movements
Fluid enough
To turn soil
Into salt

DECONSTRUCTION

for Alan and Sage

We are attempting to build more quickly
than the storm
gathering over the south ridge.
I am measuring and sawing;
he is fitting and hammering.

Through a sip of beer
he sees his daughter.
The autumn light sinks faster
than the little girl
can gather windfalls in the meadow—
button plums
and striped apples—
as many in her basket
as in her belly.

He motions her over and asks,
as she glides between the grass,
"What are the four things
necessary to build any structure?"

"Measurement, square, plumb bob, and level,"
she reports,
with neither hesitation nor embarrassment.
"Good," he grins.
"Do you know how a crowbar works?"
She bites her lip.
"You know, a lever and fulcrum?"
She shakes her braids.

He tells her to have a seat,
that these things are crucial,
and kneels down to begin simplifying the physics of construction.

I become deaf
watching his calloused hands,
paying penance for a time before she was born,
swoop and cavort
like swallows.
An opera of details
fills the space between them.

He explains
like a father with little time left.
She listens
like a daughter who knows,
eyes darting like dragonflies
simply to keep up.

JOHN THE BAPTIST

Let me tell you this
before you drown.

These waters are haunted
by the memory
of what they used to be:
just waters.

Sometimes
they tire of God's grace,
of his love,
and I cannot blame them.
Job would have
never complained
had he known of their sacrifice—
once clear and unpretentious
now thick
with the sediment of sin.

So when you stutter
your last breath,
and the current
makes a mask for your face,
understand that I will appear
as a demon above you.

You will want to surface,
and I cannot blame you.
The temptation to breathe
as you did in the womb
will be great.
Your body,
too,
is haunted
by the memory of what it used to be:
innocent.

Resist this temptation.
Salvation
has not yet learned to swim.

AMY JO SWING

APPROACH

Now that the leaves are almost gone from the trees,
the sky has come down, embracing the yellow ground,
and the woods, at least, seem greener.

The sky, then, is gray or white all the time.
The sky is anything but hesitant
now that the leaves are almost gone from the trees.

We've had one substantial snow,
only remnants left in crevices and up high,
so the woods, at least (down low) seem greener.

The gods are everywhere—in every seam,
firming up the ground and gathering us together
like the leaves which are almost gone from the trees.

There are mountains worn away to hills here
by glaciers, wind, water: roots grow through them
in the woods which, at least, *seem* greener.

Casually, I imagine, I touch your face with one finger's tip,
knowing there is no such touch as casual.
Now, when the leaves are almost gone from the trees,
and the woods at least are greener.

WHOOPING CRANE TOUR

Your absence lately has been like a companion. Strange how
the mind can hold two things at once, both true, even contrary.

Whooping Cranes mate for life and stand over five feet tall.
Black legs. Their long, white necks lift from the water,

then love changes shape and they are flying, black-tipped
wings, eight, ten feet spans: one, and then, the other.

They dig for clams, mussels, and eat them shell and all
(the calcium feeds their eggs; they will keep only one).

One of them whoops. His mate hears. First the whooping,
then his voice in the sound, then him behind the sound.
If he loves her, she must be good.

If he were you, he would be unwrapping that band on her
leg to get at the skin beneath it. They want each other. Yes.
She is leaving. Yes too.

CAPTION FOR A PHOTOGRAPH

Solstice on the ocean, on a
floating dock, eight, maybe nine
wooden hinged sections,
all floating at high tide,
all beached at the lowest tide
of the year, which is why we came—
to see the things beneath the water:
low tide zone, rocky sea creatures.

And we did see them, though we missed
the lowest tide by two days.
I've never seen you so giddy—
bent over barnacled rocks,
poking at starfish, seaweed,
tugging at bull kelp, spouting out
names as strange as their objects:
gumboot chitons, aggregate
anenome, speckled limpet.

Dragging me with my coffee
to see a sunflower star,
hubcap-sized sprawled in a shady pool.
It was grape and orange and red—
with spots and twenty-something arms
or legs. It did feel like jell-o—
you made me touch it, and I bent
down closer to see if it moved.
We must go to the ocean
every year, we agreed.

But that was all the next day—
now we are on the pier, floating.
Midnight on the longest day,
the sunlight still visible,
though the sun's below the sea.

CREATIVE**PROSE**

ARLENE **ATWATER**

NEITHER AN ENTRANCE NOR AN EXIT

Before the storm, any passerby would have seen Lamby cheerfully hanging out sheets on early spring mornings or they'd have smelled hardy stew aroma drifting through the front door of the cordwood house merrily following the forest road's grassy middle. The smell skipped leaf-to-leaf, bird-to-bird to Forte who would lift his burly head with its draping beard, sniff the air, set his ax aside and stride in heavy Redwing boots to the house, step across the sturdy porch and enter the fragrant kitchen, the humble territory of his wife Lamby LeRue. Plump Lamby lived on this land in a shy way providing crisp breads and briskly cooked stews concocted on a blue enamel woodstove and Forte supported her—his second wife and her cats—with the careful harvest of firewood from forests on LeRue land near Zimfelter's Ranch and Colt's Vegetable Farm all nestled in the timbered foothills of the Cascades.

Forte shopped for kitchen ingredients at the general store in Espacia. There, men gathered around a barrel stove on chilly mornings, glanced sideways at the rough-edged Forte pulling down canned goods and clattering them into his wire push cart, the dangerous-looking, cross-eyed glint of his left eye following the descent of each paper-labeled can. His eye was wild like that, the men from Espacia surmised, because he'd been living alone for so long always keeping that eye on the lookout for intruders and scavenging black bears. They knew he rarely left his land except to visit his son Jed on the east coast and it was on the way back from such a trip, that Forte had met his future wife on the return train. At the Espacia Station, they had stepped together from the sleeping car to the train platform opposite the general store. The Zimfelter men left the warm barrel stove to stare. Lamby's hair was in a tight braid around her fine head and she and Forte daintily picked their way to his battered, but clean pickup on that cool spring morning a year before the storm. The justice of peace married them three weeks later and that's when the LeRue woods filled with the wondrous smell of basil stew.

When the storm hit, Forte was harvesting timber and Lamby was in her kitchen. High winds skimmed across the Pacific, battered coastal foothills and the cordwood house, smashed windows and flung glass shards THUNK, THUNK into the table edge while outside Douglas-fir toppled, their root systems upright, scraggly badges of earth.

Jed flew from the east coast to assist search parties using chain saws to cut their way to the cordwood house. He was shaken, dirt-streaked, wild-eyed. He found Lamby crouched under the kitchen table, still frightened in the after-blow of the storm, holding her head in hands and swaying. Jed grasped Lamby's fleshy arms after the search crews lifted the table with its glass shards and set it by the blue stove. The Colts men in the search party pressed in with curiosity when Jed lowered plump hands from Lamby's head. Then he nestled her face and its sudden scream into his shoulder and he thought her hair lovely.

Jed LeRue is a strummer of guitar and a back-to-lander himself on sixty acres of white pine. He kept to his own, not attending his father's second marriage. But he had studied the photo of Lamby his father sent and read with interest the strange poetic words Forte wrote describing his new wife. He wrote: *she is like a violet, Jed. A violet of different colors. Lamby is shy, sprightly and reminds me of an indentation in the rich earth that needs filling up, rounding out, or shoveling in.*

As Jed held Lamby, some men swept glass. Fifty others continued tramping bristly fir and downed cedar searching for Forte. After hiring a caretaker for his sixty acres, Jed moved into his old bedroom in the cordwood house and for a time trudged acres of twisted forest searching for his father. At the house every morning he'd prepare breakfast for a grieving Lamby and over creamy oatmeal learned she had been on her way to the west coast when she'd met his father. Her husband of twenty years had died suddenly and left her near penniless. She'd vacated her apartment with its lovely four burner stove and balcony garden and caught the next train to the west coast. En route, she had spoken to Forte, attracted by his great, long beard and flashing eye. She inquired in the dining car if she might share his table, her hand resting on his sleeve. Forte easily agreed and expressed admiration of her solid, capable-looking hands.

Soon the good son had cut and stacked uprooted fir into neat piles so that the yard took on a feeling of an obstacle-filled maze and through this maze he quietly watched Lamby recover. She began to sing little tunes, her torso and arms half-twisted around porch supports. Jed would skip from wood pile-to-wood pile, protectively watching her footfalls lighten as the burden of grief lifted and when she emerged from the house one day with a basket of bedding to dry on the line, he smiled, then laughed out loud when she'd chased after the flash of a nesting Mountain Bluebird. She'd stopped in her tracks at his laughter and leaned toward him that day, her arms akimbo, a smile flitting her lips.

Lamby tilled the garden and Jed helped, relishing in her doughy, comforting hands as she guided his slim fingers to poke holes for row-after-row of small seeds. He taught her to split a stove-length log with the wedge and mall, and how to divide it CHOP CHOP CHOP with the hand ax into small kindling for her woodstove. Evenings, she unbraided her hair and they sat on the porch swing and dug their bare feet against floorboards. They pushed the swing high, then tucked their feet under and support chains slapped pleasantly in the dusk before the swing slowed smoothly to a halt. In the evening breeze, Jed sang tender guitar tunes to the fluttering of creamy, clustered Beargrass.

On a hot July night, after they'd retired, Jed walked softly in the dark across the kitchen to the door of Lamby's and Forte's bedroom. Lamby eagerly rolled to sitting, her white flannel gown twisted across her middle and one sleeve slung off her shoulder. Jed crossed the room in the fortress-like house and clasped his father's buxom wife to his chest. He lay next to her and they opened their mouths to each other. In time, Jed moved his belongings into Forte's bedroom. Lamby helped by gently hanging denim coveralls on hangers. In August, the plump stepmother stood on the porch and waited for fragrant smells from her kitchen to drift through new fast-growing firs, summoning Jed in from harvesting his father's timber.

One morning, they climbed into Forte's pickup and drove to a city two hours away. Dust from the pickup hadn't quite settled, when an airport rental coupe turned into the rutted forest road and parked near the porch. A smooth-shaven Forte LeRue stepped from the coupe. He gazed at changes in his garden and wood pile. The porch swing he and Lamby had never used, swung flirtatiously in the breeze. Memories of the storm and his stout, shy wife had returned to him only two days earlier. His fugue—caused by the fury of the storm that uprooted ancient Douglas-fir before his shocked eyes—had finally subsided after he'd wandered unknowing of home or name across the narrow top of Utah to Cheyenne then across the midwest to New York state where he worked in Buffalo at an office job he liked and was good at.

He helloed at the porch, then walked through the house he'd built. Another man's clothes filled his bureau and closet. A picture of Lamby graced one nightstand and a photo of Jed strumming his guitar smiled from the bureau. Forte stood stock-still, dumb for a moment with realization. Then he moved slowly out the door, started the coupe and parked it behind the house. His city clothes and short hair made him feel odd, distanced from a land that supported wild roses like those lightly pricking his city pant leg as he stepped from the coupe.

Back in the house, he saw a neat pile of kindling, chopped like Jed used to when he was a kid growing up in this home. From a woodpile near the kindling, Forte hefted a solid length of fir, the same fine wood he had planed, fitted, then polished to a high shine for flooring in the cordwood house. Then he sat down opposite the bedroom door, balancing the firewood across his knees.

Late that night, Jed and Lamby returned from the city. Laughing, they flung their shopping bags aside. Not bothering to light the lamp, they moved quickly to the bedroom, breathless, like they'd been waiting for this moment, this precious moment all day. Forte heard his old pickup cooling down, ticking, in the driveway and he crossed the kitchen floor. Looking out he saw the familiar truck bathed in moonlight. Behind his back, the laughing turned to groans and impatient hands unzipped and unbuttoned clothes. Forte gripped the firewood. Turning, his wild eye darted into familiar kitchen corners and he raised the wood above his head and stepped to the bedroom door.

It was then that he felt an odd disorientation, an unsureness of where he belonged. Lamby's happy murmurs danced around him and he lowered the firewood. He fingered it, felt its denseness, then bent down and positioned it firmly upright against the cordwood wall, solidly set like a bookmark tucked permanently, resolutely into a novel you never intend to reopen.

He strode across the porch, swung lightly into his pickup. Turning the key in the ignition, he flicked the headlights on, backed away and drove into the night. At the airport, he bought a one-way ticket to Buffalo. And as the jet leveled out, Forte glanced at the twinkling earth below. On that land Jed and Lamby, the cordwood house, firs, cedars and robust black raspberries would grow, shape and reshape many times. Forte turned from the land and the window and faced forward for a moment, then noted a woman across the aisle. The woman's ringless hands are dimpled and plump and as he bent toward her intending to place his hand on her sleeve, he noticed her plastic tray, like his, was down in front, ready and waiting.

ANTHONY BUKOSKI

THE VALUE OF NUMBERS

In the Navy hospital in Yokosuka, Japan, Tad Milszewski's broken leg was reset, his ribs taped, his head bandaged. The rifle company's lieutenant, who'd witnessed the accident outside of DaNang, recommended Lance Corporal Milszewski for the Purple Heart, which would be awarded him before he left Japan to complete his recuperation in the United States.

Alone in the dark hospital room, the youthful Marine felt embarrassed about the Purple Heart, knowing people would laugh when they learned what caused the wounds that would keep him on crutches so long. He was a cook riding in the back of a deuce-and-a-half when it went off one of the old French highways, leaving him pinned beneath two wash tubs and a field stove. He'd get through this, he thought, turning his attention to the nurse who'd give him his hypo. Under her watchful eye, he solved many problems that had vexed him the past three nights, such as had he done enough for his country in Vietnam and should he be embarrassed that the lieutenant's men went without a hot meal because of the accident?

When the nurse found him lifting his leg as part of his therapy, she said, "Good for you, Milszewski. Keep at it. You'll be cooking again in no time."

He counted aloud each time he elevated the shattered leg, switching to Polish after awhile. Far from home, where better to find comfort than in his parents' language? He counted, prayed, then muttered *"Jest to piekna noc . . .* This is a beautiful night" or *"Tysiace gwiazd byszcza na niebie . . .* Thousands of stars glitter in the sky." He said *"Brat i siostra,"* too, "Brother and sister."

At age nineteen, Lance Corporal Milszewki was learning certain complexities of life, one of whose ironies was that seven years before, his sister, whose name the family pronounced "Ah-nya" the Polish way, also lay in a hospital recovering from a leg operation, then later recovering at home in the East End neighborhood of Superior, Wisconsin. *Three days in Yokosuka and no letter from Anna, he thought. Now that she's better, why won't she write me?*

Drifting in and out of sleep, he remembered their dad rigging up a contraption in her room. A piece of cloth served as a sling. From it a wire cord rose to a pulley fixed to the ceiling. The cord looped over the top of the pulley then down to a metal bar with two sand-filled bags hanging from it. The bags and the bar provided a counterweight to the pressure that Anna would exert on the sling with her leg.

"Make the bags *ri-y-ce* toward the ceiling," their father said in broken English. After seven years, Thaddeus could hear them plainly, the father counting in Polish *"Raz,"* the sister responding "One."

"Dwa."

"Two."

"Trzy."

"Three."

When his parents weren't upstairs, his grandmother, whom they called *Babusia*, the aunts, or certain St. Adalbert's rosary sodality ladies were caring for her—Mrs. Sniadyak, Mrs. Adjukiewicz, Mrs. Pilsudski. Because everyone wanted to make Anna Milszewska better, two languages got mixed up in the house the way they did now when he said, "I need something to help me sleep," but, confused, told the nurse, *"Jest za zimno w pokoju . . .* It's cold in here." Knowing what the wounded need, the nurse said, "I'll be right back with your shot."

Satisfied he'd sleep, he remembered he'd been assigned times to sit with Anna, who was a year younger than him. *"Brat i siostra . . .* Brother and sister." When he should have been playing with friends or been down by the bay spying on the two herons that stood motionless in the shallows, he was watching his sister for an hour-and-a-half each spring evening until the day she was strong enough to walk. He never went into her room other times. Now in Japan, he recalled the room's beige wallpaper, the bed with the walnut frame, the brown linoleum curling along the edges of the floor. He'd hated the word "polio," hated that it was *their* house with someone sick in it. He hated to see his Ma go around the neighborhood with a canister asking for money for polio research, hated to see *Babusia* carrying pans of water upstairs to wash her granddaughter's hair, hated the way the theater stopped movies halfway through so Greer Garson on screen could request that donations be given the ushers passing by. Everyone in the place knew they were donating a dime or a nickel to help his sister, Tad Milszewski's sister, and a handful of other East End kids with polio.

When he entered her room for his evening shift, Anna would turn her head on the pillow, tighten her lips. She knew he was embarrassed of her. After five minutes, he'd say, "You should see what I did today." There ended the conversation, replaced by the scent of lilacs rising through the screen window or by the sound of their mother's clematis scraping the side of the trellis below in the spring breeze. Between them a scent of lilacs, a scraping of vines. Brother and sister.

He read from a book: "Herons and bitterns belong to a large order, which includes many notable birds such as the egrets, Maribou storks of Africa and India, and others equally as interesting."

"*Raz,*" she'd say when he did this. She'd force her leg down against the weight of the sand in the bags, continuing to count in Polish.

When she got to ten or eleven repetitions and began counting in English, he stopped reading. "You can't go *past* that in Polish? I bet you've never seen a heron either." Then he said, "How could you see the herons when you can't walk?"

"It's not important," she said, moving her Wards Airline radio closer to the bed. Those days she was like a distant song on a faraway station. Now he, Tad Milszewski, was far away from home and his leg ached. When it did, he resented the way she'd acted seven years before as though he wasn't in her room, as though he was invisible to her.

"You were talking about your sister," the nurse said.

"It's been three days. Why doesn't she write?"

"She will. I imagine she doesn't know you're here. Can you hold off a minute more on the medication? I'll be right back," the nurse said.

"I can't hold off. She hasn't written."

He stared at the ceiling, the curtains, what he could see of the shiny tile floor of the hallway. Drumming his fingers along the edge of the mattress, he recalled the sun setting behind the corner turrets of the East End fire hall, behind the chimneys of the Northern Block Building, behind the Euclid Hotel. Another spring evening without the herons because of his sister, and he was getting nervous about the pain. It was hard being ashamed of her. It was hard to go out of the house because of the shame. It was hard to have a Purple Heart under these conditions.

When the hospital quieted, the yelling of the wounded stopping, when there was no sound in the hallway now, only a dim light on and the nurse hurrying back and forth, he began to think a little differently about Anna Milszewska. Especially as time grew near for the nurse's return, he listened carefully for the sound of weights and a pulley in his sister's room. Over and over, alone in stillness, he whispered to the Blue Herons about Anna, telling them how beautiful she was to him in his hour of need, how really beautiful tonight was going to be, how easily he could count to ten despite his injured leg. He'd count higher if the nurse hurried.

At midnight, he was calling out each time he elevated his leg an inch. *"Raz, dwa, trzy,"* he was saying through the pain, realizing with each higher number what he'd been afraid of admitting: that Anna Milszewska, though younger and though once stricken with polio, was still stronger than her brother Thaddeus, who was now more insistent upon the medication.

"This will help," said the nurse when she heard him pleading for her as though she, a Navy nurse, could help him forget what he'd said to his sister about the herons years before.

"Where were you?" he asked once he'd counted to a hundred.

"You'll be all right. You'll sleep. This'll take care of you," she said.

It took a moment.

Before he drifted off, he wanted to ask her if she'd seen the Blue Herons by the bay, but the nurse left quickly. There was still no letter from Anna either, telling him she wasn't embarrassed of his wounds. Though no letter, there were a few things she'd left him to get through the night—the Polish numbers, the scraping of clematis vines on the trellis, the good scent of her hair after *Babusia* had washed it.

KARIN JACOBSON

TERRA FIRMA

And if I go
into the wild sweet of your eyes
will I know more
of this burning country I love?
                                        —*Joy Harjo*

I swing through free air, twenty feet from the top of the cliff. Above me is nothing but rock, no sign of my belayer, and below are jagged rocks and thumping lake. Instinctively, I reach for the slim purple and blue rope–the only protection I have from the ominous boulders and waves below. Why am I doing this, I wonder, as a thick ball forms in my throat?

Climbing at Palisade Head is sea cliff climbing, adventure climbing: first, you rappel down to the lake's rocky edge, then you try to climb back to the top of the cliff, where your belayer awaits. Most climbing is just the opposite: you begin at the bottom and climb to the top. Beginning at the bottom is comforting, solid ground beneath you, the visible presence of your belayer who can give advice, "beta," if you get stuck, even lower you back to the ground if you can't climb any further. At Palisade, you plunge into empty air, no solid ground in sight. As my boyfriend had warned me before I rappelled down Ex Nihlio, there are only two ways back to the top: climbing or a cold and dangerous swim down the shore of Lake Superior in search of a flat spot. There's no hidden path that you can hike up if the climb proves too difficult.

Gazing at the rock, I understand why this climb is called "out of nothing": there are no obvious holds. The rock looks uniformly sharp, gray, and steep. But grabbing the rope and dragging myself back up is not an option, so I descend slowly to the bottom of the route. When I reach the ledge that marks the start of the climb, I release the rope from my ATC, and call up to my belayer, "Off belay." Standing on terra firma, a small but solid ledge close to the lake's edge, I feel instantly at ease. It's a beautiful May day. I watch a fishing boat rocking along the waves, enjoy a cool breeze blowing my fine hair, and wait for the rope to tighten so that I can begin my ascent.

≈

The road leading to Palisade Head is narrow and winding, perhaps a warning of the sharp cliffs that await the adventurous traveler. This was my first visit to Palisade, I had driven here to meet my boyfriend of a month, Evan, for a picnic dinner. Before this, I'd heard only rumors about this menacing place—I knew, for instance, that a woman had recently committed suicide by jumping off the cliff, that some joyriding teens had sent a stolen Blazer over the cliff's edge, that a horror film had been shot here.

I met Evan in Palisade's deserted parking lot just as the October sun was setting. After we'd eaten our picnic lunch, Evan grabbed my hand and we walked toward the edge of the rocky buttress to watch the reflections of the harvest moon on the lake. Gliding down slippery rock faces, jumping over deep cracks, we hiked to a ledge over a climb called Danger: High Voltage. The bright beams of the full moon glinted on the lake's surface, turning the water into gold. The air, the water, the rock, Evan's hand in mine—everything felt full, ripe. It was a night of freedom, of a wide open vastness, no boundaries in sight. Gone was my fear of heights as we stood on the cliff's edge with no fences, no wires, no safety guards. Evan is a rock climber, so heights are his element, and his love of high places strengthened me.

"It's like we've been transported to a Hollywood set," I said. "The world in her perfection." I squeezed his hand as the harvest moon, like a spotlight, highlighted us.

"I want to make love to you on a ledge halfway down this cliff," he said.

Yes, I thought. "Yes," all of my fears stripped away by the beams of moonlight.

Then he took my hand, gently, caressing away the old tensions and stresses. The moon's spotlight shone directly on his face.

"I think I'm falling in love with you," he said.

But even on a perfect night, even in the most magical setting, a negative voice inside me whispered, "Boys always say that; he hardly knows you." All night, I'd felt this moment was a true marriage, with empty space, moon and rock to witness our vows and, in their perfection and fullness, implicitly blessing our union.

"This is a lovely moment," I answered, my fear of heights returning. Terra firma lost.

≈

How close you come to cliff's edge at Palisade. There's no separation—you stand at the edge, jump over cracks in the rock and peer into seemingly endless space. In their guide to *Superior Climbs*, David Pagel and Richard Kollath describe the cliffs as "a brooding Gothic masterpiece-sweeping buttresses of shadowed stone rise and bend between projecting turrets to complete the impossible battlement"; the rock climbs here are "steep, relentless and exposed lines." Their language invokes the almost surreal wildness of these rocks, their likeness to some fantastic, medieval fortress, or some primeval haven for dragons or other mythical beasts. But the rock isn't simply ominous: it's also beautiful. It's primary color is terra cotta, baked earth that is silver-veined and flecked with green lichen. This earth is overbaked and cracking, its deep, magnificent fissures marking the cliff's fragility, pointing to places where the present cliff is gradually stripping away from the primary rock face.

Climbing at Palisade, I'm amazed with the park's beauty, the lush trees and late summer blueberries, the vivid pinks and greens in the Precambrian rock. When we arrive on a Saturday morning in early August, the parking lot is crowded with inquisitive tourists. I walk toward cliff's edge with a huge climbing pack on my back and am asked, numerous times, "Are you climbing down that thing?" Understandably, nonclimbers think that rappelling down is the hard part, don't realize that the difficulty lies in getting back up. The tourists scare me: they walk right to the cliff's edge, leaning into empty air to watch Evan gliding down his rope to the start of a climb. I am more cautious in my viewing. I lie flat on my stomach, grip tightly whatever roots or branches are handy, then peek cautiously over the edge. Evan gracefully maneuvers up a difficult route called Palace-Aid. He uses his self-belay device, totally self-sufficient, with no belayer, just numerous, amazed onlookers. The face he climbs is covered in lichen, with no holds to be seen. Balancing on a sliver of rock, holding a dime-thin edge, hanging from a crack by his fingertips, he follows an exact and arduous sequence of moves up the cliff. It looks easy. It's not.

In the heat, the rock is greasy. As I try to match Evan's grace, my feet and fingers peel off the most secure holds–ledges, horns, thick edges–as if the rock is wiping me off its sweaty brow, wanting to be left alone on this hot summer day. But I don't feel frightened climbing today. Instead, I'm almost indifferent about whether I fall or not, hang in midair or not–I'm just climbing. When I reach the top of one of Palisade's easiest routes, Blue Bells, Evan says, "Good job."

"But I fell. A lot."

"But you made it to the top," he says. I wish I were the type of person who could be satisfied with just making it to the top, not worried about the quality of my climbing, the number of stops or falls.

Watching Evan dancing up the cliff–long lean legs easily lifting to the necessary edges; strong, accurate fingers finding the tiniest holds; body moving with the smooth grace of a gymnast–I understand what climbing is about. While I grip the rock tightly and grind my feet into it, frantic and panicked, Evan holds lightly, using the minimum amount of effort, barely touching the rock with his toes. While I cry and laugh, sweat and curse, Evan shows no sign of exertion on even the most impossible moves, pure in movement and in speech.

≈

Marge Piercy writes, "It hurts to thwart the reflexes / of grab, of clutch; to love and let go again and again." Why couldn't I tell Evan that I loved him? Why did I allow the past to infect the present? Standing in the moonlight about Danger: High Voltage, I wonder if I'll ever love without this instinctive movement toward self-protection, toward grab and clutch? I squeeze Evan's hands. Why can't I feel as if I'm on terra firma, even when I'm swinging through open air?

It's late autumn and the leaves at Palisade are changing, turning brown, edges brittle and curling. With its cyclical movements, nature is constantly revising, redoing every year, not necessarily to move toward perfection, which would be static, which would spell death, but to maintain movement and energy and beauty—in other words, magic.

≈

As I rappel over the edge of Danger: High Voltage, I remember Evan's story of how he overcame his fear of climbing. One day, he simply decided to have faith in his equipment: if you trust your rope, your gear, your harness, yourself, then what is there to fear. So this time, as I tentatively climb over the lip of the cliff, searching for firm footholds, terra firma, rather than slick, smooth faces, I focus on my equipment, on the purple and blue rope, and the metal GriGri, and my black suede shoes. I lower one foot, then another, and another, until there is no more rock: it has caved in below me and I'm gliding down through pure air, waves crashing on the rocks beneath me. As I look down into open air, my heart clenches, a fist lodges in my throat. What am I doing, I think again, I always think?

Then, strangely, I notice a tiny tree, a miniature pine, growing out of the side of the adamant rock, growing straight into the air, into the nothingness of the air, the everything of the air. My breath catches in my throat. Such freedom, such pride the pine seems to feel, pointing straight, holding its place, no barriers and no ropes, jamming its roots into the rock, just as I will soon be jamming my hands—hands and roots, equally fragile, equally strong. I place my hand into a crack, feel the smooth rock against my skin. In the past, the rock ripped at my hand, demanding pieces of flesh as penance on every climb. Now, I'm climbing hand-in-hand with the stone, as it caresses me, guiding me up the climb. Even in places where there appears to be nothing to hold onto, the rock offers me something, a tiny nugget to grab with two fingers, a minute edge for my pinky toe. I suddenly feel a vast sense of freedom, of pure openness.

Palisade Baptist Church sits at the bottom of the road, but here, at the top, is where my spirits rise. This is where I stand on the cliff's edge, with no separation between myself and open air, between myself and eternity. How do I keep this feeling of wide-openness in my life and my relationships? Can I succeed in meeting my life with hands and heart wide open? Or will my hands jam and my heart with them?

≈

Using nature as my guide, I rewrite the earlier love scene. Like a climber at Palisade, I will bravely rappel over cliff's edge, swing down through open air, and hope that I can climb back to the top.

So, when Evan takes my hand, gently caressing away the old tensions and fears, as we stand bathed in the beams of the magical harvest moon, he'll say, "I love you."

And with the ripe, full moon, and the stars, and the rocks, and the tiny pines leaning out across the lake, I'll whisper back, "I love you, Evan. I love you."

LYNN MARIA LAITALA

LESSONS I LEARNED FROM THE OLD IMMIGRANTS

Imagine a village of old men, sitting on benches in the sunshine, talking quietly in Finnish. The boardinghouses they sit in front of are weathered and in disrepair. There are children in this village, and an equal number of dogs, but it seems that even added together we are outnumbered by the old men.

There must have been other villages where immigrant men outnumbered women three to one—places where half the immigrants were men who never married, never had children or grandchildren to remember them. They were always "the boys" or "the bachelors."

I am the granddaughter of an immigrant boardinghouse. My grandmother was widowed young, so I never knew my own grandfather. But I had Oskar and Big Dave, Frank, Nick and Sippola. From these men I learned everything a child could want to learn from a grandfather. If I am dissatisfied in my life, it is only because I fail to apply the lessons they taught me.

Oskar had been living in the house when my grandparents bought it in 1913. He had a suite of two rooms upstairs—a bedroom and a sitting room with a wood cookstove where he cooked most of his own meals. Sometimes he ate porridge with us, just to be social. He kept the woodshed full of split wood for grandma. He built Auntie a wooden skiff with hand-carved oars, and comforted children.

"I'm going to run away and live with Oskar," my brother Gene threatened when he was little.

"But you can't talk to each other," Grandma said. "Oskar talks Finnish and you talk English."

"We can too talk," Gene said. "If I say *orrance*, he gives me an orange and if I say *tonus*, he gives me a donut."

In fact, we didn't need much language to learn the lessons of the old bachelors.

While they wintered in the boardinghouses in the village, many spent the warmer months in their cabins on the lake. These were beautiful log buildings with dovetailed corners, set back so they didn't mar the beauty of the shoreline. Each cabin was a little different but they all had a table at the window, a bench along the wall, a small cupboard, a narrow bed, and a wood cookstove. The simplicity, order and quiet were deeply reassuring.

"Have little, need nothing," says the old Finnish Proverb.

Every one of them had a woodshed where, besides the wood, were neatly stored tools and kicksleds and other things that they had made. There was care in details. The door handle that Nick had carved smoothly fit the hand. He built his door so solid he had to rig it with counterweights, and when you pulled it open you felt stability and security he had created in his home. The kicksleds and the boats and tools that they made were patterned on traditional styles they had learned in Finland, but each bore the stamp of the individual craftsman. The bachelors were, every one of them, craftsmen.

The old Finnish proverbs say, "If you can't make it, you don't need it," and "Making it—great pleasure, buying it none."

These men had come to America with high hopes of earning money and buying land here or back in Finland, of marrying and raising families—and none of it had happened as they hoped. They were paid poorly and treated badly in industrial work. The Winton mills and logging camps that employed them had shut down in 1920, leaving them to move on or survive from the resources at hand.

Their life experience made them deeply suspicious of power and authority, which was invariably at odds with cooperation and common sense. They did not recognize status based on money or position. Status derived from character and skill, expressed through work. Thirty years after he worked in a logging camp, Big Dave was still esteemed on Fall Lake because he had been a great teamster in the logging camps, handling a four-horse hitch pulling tons of logs with ease. He made his living as a guide after the logging ended. Big

Dave was quick to educate people who mistook a guide for a servant. Once a tourist handed him a cup and told Big Dave to get him a drink. Big Dave simply dropped the cup in the lake. The guide was the expert, and a tourist had better show respect. You don't let other people define who you are.

A few of the old Finnish bachelors drowned themselves in disappointment over their lives, but it was so rare that explanations were made for angry or self-pitying men. The bachelors I admired found joy and endless adventure in the world around them, following the seasons fishing, hunting, trapping, picking berries. In the small piles of rusting cans in the pits in the woods back of the cabins, Gene and I found evidence that they partied, too.

Women could still make problems for the old boys. On our part of the lake, only Waino had a wife. Linda was simple, and it was whispered that she had a past, but Waino was very proud of her—and very jealous. She painted her cheeks bright red and permed her blond hair to a fine frizz. Waino carved every one of her perm rods by hand, and rolled her hair on them himself. One time he took a notion that Big Dave had been visiting his Linda while he was out on the trapline. He rowed the half-mile along the shore to Big Dave's cabin, shouting curses and threats, forewarning Big Dave. Fortunately for Big Dave, his cabin had a rocky shore. He pitched the rocks at Waino as he stood shouting in his rowboat, and repelled the attack.

Waino sought revenge by turning Big Dave in to the authorities because Big Dave had been in the country 45 years without getting naturalized. The authorities were indeed horrified to discover that Big Dave was living hand to mouth without pension and signed him up for Social Security.

Being able to tell a good story counted a lot among the old bachelors, and a good story couldn't be told too many times. They told stories about the odd and funny and awe-inspiring things they saw out in the woods or on the lake. Here is one of Villi's stories:

"I had a dog I liked a lot. He was a good dog, but then he started chasing deer. You know, you can't have a dog chasing deer, but I liked that dog so much I couldn't bear to shoot him. One day

I heard him barking and barking in the woods. The snow was extremely deep, so I had to snowshoe out to where he was barking. I took my gun like I always did. I followed the barking and found my dog. He had cornered a deer. She was too exhausted to flounder through the deep snow anymore, or even to dodge my dog in the little area they had packed down. My dog moved closed and closer, slashing near her heels. I shot my dog. The doe just stood there a minute. Then she walked toward me and knelt down a few yards away. It was a bow. She was thanking me. Then she walked past me into the woods."

The old bachelors worked in the woods, mostly by trapping, making a living from their intimate knowledge of animals, land, water, weather. The nature they talked about was neither harmonious nor brutal. It was all things. Glory and horror. Abundance and starvation. No two seasons alike, no two days alike. Intricacy, complexity, diversity, power. They loved the challenge. They never lost their sense of wonder. They created their own harmony by practicing a code of ethics as old as man himself: take only what you need, never waste, kill quickly, leave breeding stock, have respect. As man's ally, Villi's dog was bound by the same code.

The old men believed that if they practiced those ethics, nature would reciprocate, and yield what he needed to survive. And it did. They lived well because they got pleasure from their work and had few needs. It satisfied Villi profoundly to live so directly from Creation. When the doe thanked him for killing his dog, she confirmed the code he lived by, and confirmed his sense of mystery and wonder in Creation.

When they were young, all the Winton Finns belonged to the Industrial Workers of the World, trying to change the world into a better place so that they could lead good lives. Perhaps they were not so much trying to change the world, as to hold on to values that had served well in the old agrarian world they knew—values of cooperation and mutual aid. People helped each other out. Men took care of widows and children. You got no respect or prestige if you bettered yourself taking advantage of somebody else.

They didn't succeed in introducing those values to industrial

America, but they still cooperated among themselves. They had given up the struggle to change the world long before I knew them. As old men, they quietly found good in what life offered in the here and now.

This is the good they found: the ability to create, to work, to cooperate, to have a good time, to be endlessly fascinated by the oddities and mysteries of the natural world. To live in peace with themselves.

I know now that they had to struggle to make peace with their own lives. I knew them after they had succeeded, and I only glimpsed the hard journey my old bachelors made. So well had they reconciled themselves to the turn of fate that destroyed their youthful hopes that I did not believe that there was any other life the old bachelors would have rather lived. Maybe I was wrong.

One evening I sat with Auntie and Big Dave on the log we used for a bench, a little up the hill from the shore. Big Dave broke the friendly silence, speaking Finnish. "Translate," I said to Tati, as always. She thought awhile and chose her words carefully.

"When the light wanes on the ebbing waves, my heart fills with old yearnings."

But I think that they would rather be remembered by the note scrawled on the wall of Big Dave's cabin: "November 24. Big Dave and I went whitefishing. Got 32 whitefish and 2 tulippes. Fell in. Got drunk. Had a good time."

MARGI PREUS

A FISH STORY

What he dreamt about were fish. In his dreams trout streams ran fast and hard, the water like pulse beats. There were trout as big as Luciano Pavarotti, and northern pike with teeth like sewing needles.

The problem, in life as in his dreams, was that he could never catch any of them.

So it was either give up fishing or get better lures.

He stared past dangling icicle Christmas lights into the window of the sporting goods store as if gazing into a jewelry store. . .so many gem-like baubles, sparkling and glistening like pendants and earrings. His heart pressed against his breast pocket so hard he could feel the needle-nosed pliers he kept there biting into his skin.

There was a woman in that store. . . well, a creature—a beautiful creature--who had no legs. At least, he'd never seen them, though he'd tried. She was always behind a counter. It was disconcerting to look at her because her eyes changed color the way lakes do with the weather, from windy-day green to white-sand-bottom blue. If he had been given to flights of fancy, he would have suspected she was not human at all, but a mermaid. This was a thought that never would have occurred to him before—even he knew it— if it hadn't been for the dreams.

He sucked in his stomach and pushed open the door, stepping onto the sea-foam green carpeting. Except for a hum that sounded like a small outboard motor off in the distance, the place was silent.

Past the basins seething with slick black leeches and glimmering shiners, he saw her. She was seated behind a counter, untangling a reel of 20 lb. test.

What was it he was going to say? "I can't catch any fish. I need something foolproof, to reverse the tragic circumstance of my life?" That? Or, how about: "Could you come out from behind that counter so I can see your legs?"

She glanced up. Her eyes, he noticed, were the color of a lake with lots of chop. Flecked with white foam, the tiny white caps indicating good fishing.

"Can I help you?" she said.

He considered that. He wondered. It seemed for a moment that she could; she really could help him. But then, no. He was swimming under way too much ice and he had no idea where the air hole might be.

He stalked over to the counter and spun a rack of hand-tied flies around. "Angie," her name tag said. She was nice looking, he thought, and very petite. Short was the word.

Marlon moved over to the raincoats and scraped the hangers along the rack. "Uh, Miss?" he said, "I have a question about this jacket." He turned; she was not behind the counter, she was no-where; she'd disappeared.

"Yes?" It was her voice. "Can I help you?"

A quarter turn. She wasn't there. Another quarter. Still not there. Marlon turned all the way around twice, then looked down and saw her. She didn't have legs, as it turned out; not legs like Marlon could relate to; they were misshapen as driftwood and even less useful. She was seated in a wheelchair.

"Oh!" The word escaped unexpectedly. He felt his heart leap and then settle far down, somewhere between his in-soles and his polypropylene socks.

She laughed. "Sorry if I startled you. Just greased the bearings on this thing—runs pretty smooth."

"Oh–ha!" he laughed, sort of. Then, nothing. He felt this well of disappointment in his gut. Along with relief. He wouldn't have to fall in love with her after all. It would be simpler that way.

"What were you wondering?" she asked.

He stammered for awhile. "–I was just wondering–uh," He felt like an idiot. No, he thought, I *am* an idiot. I can't catch fish. I can't fall in love with regular people. And I'm an idiot.

"How did you come to work here?" he said. "Do you fish?" What a ridiculous question!

"It's my dad's business. I never thought I'd work in it, though. I wanted to be a ballerina when I grew up–can you believe it?"

"That's nothing," he said, "I wanted to be a poet!" he snorted and realized he'd never told anyone that before.

She stared back at him and didn't laugh. "Well, what's stopping you?"

"Well!" he said, as if it were obvious, as if anyone could see his handicap: his poor, dull brain. He noticed a tie on the rack behind her that had tiny fish all over it. How long had it been since he'd said anything to her? He looked at her; her eyes now dusk-lavender.

"I'll take that tie—the one with the fish all over it," He pointed; she turned. "And you. Would you like to go fishing?" he said. (Had he said that?) She turned back, the fish tie in her hand, and looked at him with flat calm eyes.

"Anything else?" she said. (Good. I didn't really say it.)

"Uh, no, that'll be it."

He wondered how this tie was going to help him catch anything.

"What do you fish for?" she said.

"Whatever's biting," His standard answer to the question, then added, "Only it seems like nothing ever is."

"Where?"

"The big lake, mostly. Big lake, big fish," he wiggled his eyebrows. "So they say."

"I just heard a beautiful story," she said, looping the tie into a box, "about how the fish came to be in the big lake. Long ago the lake was as beautiful as it is today, but it was barren. There were no fish in it. There was a village of native people who lived on the game they found in the woods and they used the lake for water, that was all. A white trader came to the village and a native girl fell in love with him. One day, when he came to the village she felt sure he had finally come to ask her father for her hand, and she dressed in a pure white deerskin dress, her best beaded moccasins, combed her glossy black hair 'til it shone and went to meet him. But he had only come to say goodbye. He was going back to his wife and family in Montreal. She was so heartbroken; she thought her life was over.

She threw herself off a cliff into the big lake, and drowned." Angie stopped and placed the top on the box.

"That's it?" he said.

"No. Did you want that gift-wrapped?"

"Uh, no." He waited for her to go on. She reached under the counter and pulled out a bag and slid the box into it. "After the girl drowned," Angie went on, "her skin began to peel away, but as it peeled, it flickered off—fish! The shreds of her skin became thousands of silvery whitefish, her hair became trout, her gleaming nails turned to salmon. Her eyes became agates, her teeth shells. And her spirit, I guess, went into the water."

A steelhead flashed past in Marlon's brain and he felt sweat start up on the back of his neck. That was it! That was what he wanted—had been trying—to catch—those small flashes, that spirit, whatever the heck that was. It wasn't fish at all. But he didn't say that. What he said was, "Don't you think that's kind of creepy?"

Angie looked up, a shimmering trail of moonlight glinting just out reach in the lake of her eyes. "No. I like the thought of all that beauty coming from tragedy."

"Ah," said Marlon. He'd have to think about that.

"It's kind of selfish, but I even like to think that something beautiful will come from my own little tragedy, somehow."

"But you—" Marlon stopped, thought what to say instead of what he was going to say, but she was staring at him with her drop-off deep eyes, and he said it anyway, "—you are beautiful."

She laughed a charming laugh, the sound of tiny toy bells far-away, on a mountain in Switzerland somewhere, and Marlon thought the laugh beautiful, too.

"That's kind of you," she said, ". . .I wasn't really referring to my disability." Angie leaned across the counter as if to say something confidential. Her hand rested on the counter in front of him, palm up.

He resisted the urge to put his hand in it and instead stared at it blankly.

"How do you want to pay for this?" she said.

Marlin let out a little yip-like laugh and reached for his wallet.

Angie slid his card through the machine and handed Marlon the slip to sign. "What kind of fishing did you have in mind?" she said.

So, he had said it after all. Marlon glanced out the window at the snow falling slant-wise in the glow of the streetlight. "Ice fishing?"

"Sure," she said and handed him a shopping bag w/the tie in it.

Marlon would construct a handicapped accessible dark house for spear fishing. He'd wheel her across the slick, black ice past patches of snow. The wind would send swirls of it smoking across the ice. The house would have two bright holes shining in the floor and the two of them would sit staring down into the light. Fish would dart by, little ones, shiners, or a northern might glide by, and snap that decoy up with its teeth.

Marlon plunged back into the dark night. The cold air swirled around like water. His bare head stung, as if he'd just dove from a great height.

YVONNE RUTFORD

FRYBERGER WOODS

On my wall at home hangs a framed photograph, an eleven-by-fifteen print that shows in the foreground the old brick and wrought iron gate at the entrance to Fryberger Woods. The photo was taken on a misty autumn day; wet yellow leaves are strewn along an asphalt trail, once a driveway but now broken bits of black rubble, its width narrowed by encroaching grasses, curving out of focus toward the old stone bridge over Tischer Creek. The photograph is the only tangible picture I have of Fryberger gate, a portal leading inward to the vivid mental pictures of my childhood wilderness.

Most distant in my memory is an image of my brother and me—I couldn't have been more than four, he, seventeen months older—following my parents through those woods. At the top of the steep hill on the other side of the creek was a root cellar, maybe, or an old chicken coop, I'm not sure. My memory sees it in black-and-white, not color, the black-and-white of old horror films. A gray concrete structure rising just above the tangled brush and tall grass, moss-covered and crumbling in decay, black squares of windows breathing the cold dark damp of earth. My father, sensing the fear in two young children, seizing the opportunity to assure us it was indeed haunted, daring us to enter its dark cave.

Clearer and brighter, color images now, I'm a few years older and explore Frybe's Woods with my brother. At the top of a hill our backyard turns to woods, and a trail drops steeply, wet and rocky, through the trees to the creek. Frybe's Woods is across Columbus Avenue, but we can get there under the bridge. Wading through the creek with empty Folger's coffee cans in hand, the water draws us into the woods. We spend whole afternoons on the remains of a tree that has fallen into the water and in its decaying state reveals driftwood lines and ridges that echo the eddies of the creek itself. From this log we watch water bugs skitter across the stream's surface and dip our silvery cans into the brown water to catch minnows and gaze at this other-world life.

1967. Amy moves in next door. Tall and pretty, brown hair, blue eyes, and freckles, she's a treasure: a girl, my age, with my sense of adventure. Amy and I explore deeper into the woods, stretching our independence. Frybe's touches the boundaries of our yards, stretches just four square blocks, but to us it's a vast wild place. And always explored from the creek, the water again drawing us in, not from its azure forget-me-not fringed banks but immersed in its cold stream. We feel the water rush past our ankles where it bubbles clear over gravel beds, and stir up dark ooze from the bottom of still pools, silt settling into our tennies. We stand upon small islands created where the creek bed has split, and feel triumphant in this place reached only by water.

Amy has "water tennies" and I envy her. Water tennies are spare shoes, shoes replaced by new ones while they're still in good enough shape to be worn exploring creeks. My family's in a different economic bracket; my mother mixes powdered milk to save money feeding four kids and won't take us to Sears for new shoes until the ones we have are disintegrated. I have to explore the creek in my only pair of tennies, and risk getting in trouble when I get home.

But that's hours away, maybe my mother won't notice the muddy shoes if I slip in through the garage door, I don't have to worry about it now, because for now we're adventuring. Frybe's is like a huge house with many rooms and we disappear among them. From the shaded creek, we explore over land, tracing ancient footpaths, discovering secret gardens, climbing the steep hill to upper Frybe's, where the sidewalks and driveway of a bygone farm are being reclaimed by wildflowers. We scratch our arms on raspberry thorns, bruise our shins on boulders, and in the evening emerge, our feet translucent white and wrinkled from the long day spent in creeks and wet woods.

As a teenager once I walked through Frybe's with my mother, beneath the canopy of elms over Waverly Avenue, down Hardy Street, across Columbus Avenue, past the old gate and into the woods. In a rare moment when my mother revealed her emotions, spoke to me as a friend not a parent, she said simply, "I don't know how you feel, but I can't imagine ever living anywhere but this neighborhood." It was an awkward moment; as a young teenager I was ill-prepared to share with my mother this way, but I sensed an importance to it.

"I love it here too, Mom." A connection, however fleeting, between mother and daughter through shared love for a place.

Those days, those seasons, those years etched the image of Frybe's Woods forever in my mind. Of course, I didn't think about these mental pictures then, didn't think they would ever be all that remained of Frybe's. Frybe's would always be there.

In my late twenties, my visits to the old neighborhood were limited to family gatherings at the red house on Waverly, where my parents still lived, where I could still hear car tires rattle the manhole cover on Arrowhead Road, where some of the neighboring homes had new occupants but many still housed neighbors who had been there for decades. This was a place where I could count on things not having changed. On rare occasions, my brothers, sister and I took our own kids on walks through Frybe's to stretch our legs after a holiday meal, and to reminisce. Frybe's Woods was as much a constant, as much a given, as my parents' house was.

Around this time memory began to slip away from my mother. Alzheimer's set in and bit by bit erased the roots of her life. By the time I neared forty, she required full-time care, and my father cared for her at home, her home since 1962, maybe the only place in her lost world that remained familiar to her. I stayed with her for a few days last spring while my father was out of town. Although her mind was faded, my mother was still tall and strong and able to walk, and one day we walked again through the old neighborhood and past the old gate, back into Frybe's Woods . . . my mother's loss of memory bringing me back to my deeply etched memories of Frybe's.

What I didn't remember from childhood were the details of

the woods' natural beauty. Slipping into those woods, I heard only the distant whir of a lawnmower or the echoing bounce of a basketball in some driveway to remind me I was really in a city. Venturing inward, town sounds were washed over by the trickle of the creek, the rustle of young leaves on ancient trees, and bird songs filtering down from high in the canopy. Ovenbird, vireo, veery. The ground beneath our feet was lush with forget-me-nots, ferns, and fragrant lily-of-the-valley, and the very same well-worn footpaths that I traveled throughout childhood. I remembered every trail and still, after twenty-five years, knew them by heart. The only change that had occurred here was subtle, natural.

I don't know whether those trails traced their way into my mother's memory, whether she remembered at all the decades of walking kids and dogs through those woods in that neighborhood she once couldn't imagine ever leaving. But she seemed to enjoy being there, and that was enough.

Holding this fresh view and refreshed memory of the woods as unchanged after all those years–holding the realization that the same footpaths I remembered from childhood were still there and a sense of comfort that they would always be there–I learned within weeks of that walk with my mother that Fryberger Woods was slated for development into residential housing.

Now, on a summer day while minnows dart in Tischer Creek, while breezes brush the leaves of the ancient maples along its bank, utility crews dig into the soil of Fryberger Woods to lay water and sewer lines.

Among my childhood scrapbooks I have a school project–9th grade biology, October 1974–a collection of leaves pressed against pages of a booklet, the trees labeled by their common and Latin names. I remember doing that project, with Amy, gathering those leaves in Frybe's Woods. Paper birch, weeping birch, river birch. Black ash, mountain ash. Red, silver, and sugar maple. Box elder and bur oak. Northern white cedar, red pine, white pine; black, blue, and white spruce. American elm and willow. Tamarack and crab apple. Twenty-seven-year-old fragments sealed in clear contact paper, remnants of a diverse forest now uprooted and lost.

My sister says to me, go to Frybe's, go see it, see what remains.

I have vowed never to return there. There are places so much a part of our being, so precious, so much within us, these places become "permanent"–even though logically we know they're not, we can't accept the idea of their destruction. Frybe's Woods was home to my childhood, a sacred place. It is a landscape too precious in my memory, too much a part of me, to witness its destruction.

Recently I dreamed Columbus Avenue was a river. Milky greenish water, like a glacial stream. Deep and swift. I was being carried by its current. But at the entrance to Frybe's something happened to the current. A stronger current pulled me from the main stream, carried me past the old gate, carried me back to Frybe's Woods.

There I will hold Frybe's . . . in the fluid depths of my dreams, flowing through my memory, and in a single photograph on my wall of the old gate, open, drawing me back.

CAITLIN TAYLOR

BREATHING

All of my children are breathing.

For a period of time some years ago, it was my only requirement of them.

We experienced about five excruciatingly difficult years, and the birth of the requirement was slow. I fought and fumed and worried and cried first. I clamped down on what they were. Battled with what they weren't. Pleaded and begged and yelled and demanded and threatened and swore.

One evening, I had what seemed a soul-questing conversation with my son. The summer night was mild. We lived above a frowzy Chinese restaurant, and had a room-sized balcony porch, where we sat. His voice was pressed down as we talked. His blue eyes gazed out at unseeable distances. My blue eyes gazed in at unseeable distances. My heart squirmed and worried, as I felt for answers to his unanswerable questions. I admitted my ignorance about the meaning of life. I sighed with his sigh. I stroked his hand, and ruffled his hair. This child took to physical affection. When my words and my limited wisdom did not have the answers, sometimes my touch did. I loved him simply. He was my son, my progeny. Like thousands of sons and daughters through the cascade of history, a simple vibrant link to all that is holy, all that is of import, all that imbues life.

The talk wound down. I kissed his lightly furred cheek, and said goodnight. He took a notebook, a rope, and a pen, and hoisted himself over the raingutters, onto the slope of roof above the balcony. He sat on his haunches, opened the notebook, and looked out into the vast, impenetrable night.

I smiled up at the sight of him, before ducking into the house. I loved how nature drew him. I loved his nimbleness and proclivity for odd spaces. I shook my head and sighed. I felt hopeful. Happy.

Knew all the talk was some sort of omen that he would find his way. An hour for the two of us allowed, at least, some communion. No hurry. No commotion. A gift hour. An oasis in the blast of our struggling life.

I didn't miss him in the morning.
Sleeping late is endemic to teenage life.
It was after lunch sometime. I went to roust him out, and found the empty bed. A mild jolt fed through me. What? Where?
"Jeroll?" I called.
No answer. Just as I'd had no answer for him the night before. I strolled out to the balcony. Looked around. Called again. My mind buzzed, whirred, clicked. I thought of my last sight of him: small smile, thoughtful, gazing out.
I thought of the notebook and of the pen. I thought of the rope. The rope? Why a rope?
I thought of the second roof that stepped up from the first one. I thought of the chimney, and the trap door he'd found up there, that let into the attic. The locked attic.
The whirring in my brain increased.
I thought of the notebook and of the pen. I thought of the mild despair as he pressed for some meaning in life.
And I thought of the rope.
I thought of how very late in the day it was. Very late to be sleeping. Even for a teenager.
I thought I'd need a ladder, being not so nimble as he.
My breath left me as I navigated the stairs. The nightmare of my thoughts made a whirlwind in my brain as I burst into the neighbor's shop. Words to ask for a ladder fought to find breath and shape. Cottonmouth teamed with wide eyes, as I tried to make a simple request.
While in my brain I thought of only one use for pen and paper.
While in my brain I thought of only one use for rope.
Ten wooden rungs put me over the edge. I made my way quickly—teeth clamped, breath clamped, eyes brimming. Steeling

myself, I gulped air as fingertips slid over gritty roof tiles and sneakered feet found purchase.

I saw the rope first, wound about the chimney. Then I saw his wavy hair, lifting in a light breeze. His prone body stretched out from there, arms slack, face expressionless. The rope looped his waist, not his neck.

The first relief was a cold one. I swung a leg over, and found a spot to kneel on the small flat surface beside the chimney. I shouted his name. I grasped the cool arm, and shook him.

Not even a groan.

I shook harder. "Jeroll! Jeroll! Jeroll!" through a rigid jaw. Tears spilled, and I slapped at his chest. I grasped the second shoulder and shook him again, angry now. "Jeroll!"

Then the moan.

The groggy, petulant rasp, "What? What?" The eyes struggling open, then closing again.

"What are you DOING here?"

"Sleeping."

"Sleeping?"

"Mmnmph." And the head rolled on a slack neck. He dove back into sleep, deep and sweet, leaving me kneeling next to sky.

I backed my fanny up to the sturdy brick of chimney. Tipped my head back, and let the tears flow. My right hand found his left arm and stroked up and down, up and down—finding the live warmth beneath the skin's cool.

I looked at him breathing.

And that's when I came up with the only rule: Be breathing in the morning.

Where there is breath, there is life. Where there is life, there is hope.

I would never forget it.

When he woke truly, I got the whole story. He only wanted the adventure of sleeping high up. The rope's only purpose was to secure him at his zenith, not to deprive me of mine. I had given him my addiction to sleeping in open air. In the midst of stars, instead of beneath them, was his own variation on a theme.

With the chimney at my back, and relief flooding warmly through me, I enjoyed my own time at the top. It seemed a secure height from which to count my blessings. For the moment, I blessed even the struggle that was such potent proof of life. A struggle that sometimes made us all wish for death. I was no stranger to the wish myself. Perhaps the new rule should apply to me, too.

In that comic way life has of turning things upside-down, I, the rescuer, found myself in need of rescue. Adrenalin and that visceral mother-response had zoomed me nearly effortlessly to the summit my son had climbed on purpose.

One distinct difference between that son and I, is that he is natural-born mountain goat. I am not.

So, he coached me.

"A little to the left now, Mom. That's right. Slow and easy. You're doing fine, Mom. Just don't look down! There now, a little further. You're almost there, Mom. You're almost home."

By the time we hit terra firma–if blacktopped balcony can be so termed–I clasped his shoulder and said, "Good thing you were alive. I might never have got back down without you."

He reached around me with those cool strong arms, and locked me in a young man's hug. A son's hug.

It's hundreds and hundreds of mornings later, now. And he is still obeying the rule.

Hope abounds.

COLIN KEITH THOMSEN

SNOWBANK

The day begins with a shock, the sudden, wretched screaming of the alarm. I can feel the tired in my fingers, in my ankles, in my eyes. In my head which aches and pleads for a cup of coffee. Impossibly I excavate myself from beneath the blankets and start across the room to satisfy the alarm. The carpet beneath my feet is saturated with frigid water. By the window frame, the cheap plaster has given way to the weight of the melting snow, and water oozes through the split seam then down the wall, staining it brown. I put on my robe and start looking for the duct tape.

Outside my window it's late February, the dead of winter. My neighborhood has somehow been passed over for snow removal and the sidewalks are an impassable combination of thick ice and standing water. The snow isn't light, powdery or pure anymore, it's thick and crystalline, but melty and soaks everything instantly, soaks through your boots, your socks, turns your feet blue. The snowbanks in retreat suck up and reveal four months' worth of garbage and road sand, dyeing the whole neighborhood in dishrag gray.

It's 7:23. That makes about two hours of sleep. I've been keeping late nights, perpetually occupied with school work, getting ready to leave the country, and trying to complete a feature story for a local alternative newspaper. The article itself is not challenging to write but the subject matter—which involves domestic violence— is extremely taxing emotionally. It's difficult to shuffle through the darkest chapters of peoples' lives, giddily excerpting the worst parts for the purposes of a piece of writing. The heroic people I interview are cooperative, even eager to have my attention, but it feels vulgar.

Late for class, I dash out of my apartment to catch a bus. As I scurry to to the bus stop, a man, screaming, passes me, headed the opposite direction. I keep my eyes glued to the pavement, eager to avoid acknowledging him and thus inviting further interaction.

Ain't no woman beat me yet! he shouts. Ain't no woman gonna hit me around...

Passing him, I look up. I freeze.

There's a woman, with a cane and a brace that runs up her leg, collapsed, on her side, in the snowbank. She is shouting, at the man. I cannot feel my limbs.

The man turns now, to shout back at the woman, and there I am, caught between them, as they scream at each other. It's savagely cold and the wind is ripping across 24th Street as this woman lies collapsed in the snowbank.

The wind conjures tears from my eyes, which streak back across my face. I rush to the woman's side. I ask is she all right? Does she need some help? She shouts, at the man, but her words come fast and slurred. I cannot understand them. I hear only the volume. Then, suddenly there's the man, standing right there.

Sorry sir, he says. Excuse me. Sorry you had to see this. He motions for me to move on. I take one step back, but stay close. He leans toward the woman. To hurt her? To kill her? I am not really here, this, this is not. Me. Me. I can see the man is strong underneath his bar jacket and he's drunk and am I going to fight him or hold him back? I am one hundred and fifty pounds of bone and skin between this man and violence. I am not really here, I'm just adrenaline, and my limbs moving and words coming out of my mouth and the second between the lightning and the thunder. Lasts *forever*.

Then a passerby, a younger woman, approaches. The man turns away as though to leave. This second woman is able to understand the woman in the snowbank. Together, we gingerly pick her up and place her on her own feet. She sighs, and the alcohol in her breath smells like burning neoprene. The man is back, thanking us, apologizing. We stand guard at the woman's side. They exchange words.

I'm through with you, woman, I love you, but y'ain't never gonna push me around again.

Fuck you! She tries feebly to hit him with her cane, then shoves him, hard, forcing herself back to the snowbank. More shouting. Again, the man turns as though to leave.

We gotta do something, I whisper to the other woman. She shrugs, gets back into her car. I step in front of it. She rolls down the window. Do you have a cell phone? Do we call the cops? Do these people need to go to jail?

It's probably their everyday way of life, she says. They're drunk, they're fighting. But look, anyway—she indicates approaching police that I do not see. We did what we could, she says, then drives away. The confidence is not mutual.

I stand there in the road for a long second, lost in my little corner of these two people's lives. I look into the faces of the spectators who I now realize have been watching the whole time—teenage girls at the bus stop, little kids, old people passing by—for guidance. Just me, center stage, no idea what to do.

The man is back. He bends to her, speaking softly now, his face to her face. He places a kiss on her forehead. Then he's gone, for good.

She stays there in the snowbank.

A car pulls up. Opening doors, pointing fingers. The police? My bus arrives. Reluctantly I get on.

Half an hour later, I'm at school, ignoring the professor, wringing my hands and staring across the room at a sorority girl. She's wearing a sweatshirt with her greek letters embroidered in pink, pink that matches her nail polish.

When I come home, everyone's long gone. Just a divot in the snowbank, dirty with cigarette butts and road sand.

SUSAN NIEMALA **VOLLMER**

OPENING DAY

Ignoring his bum hip, my father is the first one down the muddy riverbank, as eager as a kid to be on the water. The aluminum canoe is so cold that it burns our bare fingers, and we hurry to pass it hand over hand down to the gray river. By tradition, the fishing opener is raw and chilly, reminding us that it hasn't been long since the ice left the lakes.

Although he faithfully buys a fishing license each spring, my father hasn't been out for the opener for several years. He immediately reverts to his fishing guide past as he crisply instructs my husband, sister, and me where to load the tackle boxes, landing net, rods and thermos bottles in the canoe and boat.

We have no way of knowing that this will be his last fishing opener, that a heart attack will take his life, come October. We only know the camaraderie of the day. My sister and I remind each other of the long childhood evenings spent out here with our father in Grandpa's boat, swatting pesky mosquitoes and soothed by Lifesavers from Daddy's pocket.

In a few weeks, the little black sand flies will be out by the thousands, and mosquitoes will hover and whine near the reeds. For now, the wind snakes along, following the shape of the river. It skims over the crusty patches of snow that still lie in the shaded hollows and picks up an icy breeze that nips our exposed wrists and sneaks under the backs of our tightly zipped jackets.

We jockey our boats into position, following the unspoken rules that keep us a proper distance from the other fishermen hunched pensively over their rods. My father, carrying a map in his mind's eye, drops anchor by the old walleye hole.

This is his river. As a child, he and his brothers played, swam, and fished here. They chased crayfish through the shallows, and carried stringers of walleyes home through the dusty streets. The old wooden boathouses are gone, the noisy metal bridge replaced, but he still knows this river.

Nobody talks much. Conversations come in one and two word sentences.

"Bite?"

"Naah–snag."

The wind whistles the river's song as casting lines sing, plop, and are slowly reeled back in. There is little other movement except in the eyes of the fishermen, watching the lines and bobbers of the others as closely as they watch their own.

As always, my father hoists the first fish. Not a keeper, it glints silver momentarily in the thin sunshine. The river claims it back. Near the opposite shore, there is brief excitement as a man nets a two foot northern. We make a few envious comments as we fillet it with our eyes.

We float on the river, our eyes mirroring the clouds overhead. Time loses all meaning. An ancient Ojibway canoe could round the bend. We might spot the boat of my immigrant grandfather, who carried the forests and lakes of Finland in his blood, and fished this river well into his eighties. Our unborn children could be dropping lines into the water, and peering delightedly into the depths of this constant, ever-changing river.

I endure good-natured razzing when we have to pull into the shore so that I can disappear behind a handy spruce tree. The cold wind offers a sufficient excuse. It is too early for my husband and me to tell the others that I am carrying a child who will arrive during the coldest week in January, a child who may one day fish this same river.

Restlessness seizes the group. The company around us changes frequently as everyone hunts for the best fishing spot. Boats start with roars and move away. Fishermen pull their hats more snugly over their ears and parry for new positions. The rivalry is silent, not hostile, but solidly present.

With shivering legs and numb fingers, we finally concede defeat to the river. We awkwardly drag and curse the metal boats onto the shore. They bump heavily against our legs, turning our fingers into reddened icicles.

The leather bar stools feel warm and comfortable after the hard seats. Our voices thaw as our glasses make wet circles on the polished bar, toes tingling on the brass rail. I pretend to sip my drink, pass it over to my husband. It isn't necessary. The laughter and the old stories are enough to fill me with a river of warmth.

LOU KILLIAN ZYWICKI

THE BENEDICTION

I grew up in a world of clear blue skies, plunging ore mines, towering Norway pines, and frigid winters on the Mesabi Iron Range in northern Minnesota. My community was tight, loving, and limited. From age twelve to age nineteen I attended school on the same city block. When I finished junior high school I crossed the street to the high school, when I finished high school I crossed back again to the junior college attached to one end of the junior high. When I wasn't in school I worked in my family's business, was with one of my many cousins, spent time with my family, or was in church.

We were a small town dotted with churches. My particular church taught us to know the Bible, to know that God and our families loved us, to put God in the center of our lives, and to prevail against dances, movies, alcohol, smoking, and any other dangers that would lead us down the path to hell. All this I endorsed without question.

The fall of 1967, the week before my twentieth birthday, I left for the University in Duluth, Minnesota. I was armed with my faith and surrounded by close friends, the walls of protection were left at home.

This new world was a heady, sweet wine. As an English major I had found my heaven. I had new friends who sat in coffee houses until the early hours writing poetry and short stories. I acted in plays that entertained massive audiences. I met people who loved the same books I did and who could discuss them for hours.

It was in one of these late night sessions that I met Sandy, and when we began the long, frosty walk back to our rooming houses we discovered that Sandy had a room in the house next door to where my friends and I roomed. Soon Sandy was a part of our group, joining us as we studied or cooked supper together.

Sandy's intelligence had won her a full scholarship and the

shining smile on her freckle-filled face drew people to her. Sandy's sharp blue eyes and quick laughter gave no clue to the secrets she was hiding. She seemed to walk comfortably in the world and again and again I used her as my guide as I learned to move beyond my protected upbringing.

When we completed the first university play of the season I was afraid to attend the cast party because I was sure I wouldn't fit in. I had never been in a room with people who were drinking and smoking. Sandy laughed at my fears, and went to the party with me. I soon learned that I could have fun with many kinds of people without compromising my strict upbringing or being judgmental.

Soon we were challenging each other to try new things. We rented skis and laughed until we ached as we attempted our first run down the ski hill. She stood back stage and cheered me on the first time I gathered up the courage to read my poetry at the coffee house. When my roommates and I decided to leave the rooming house and rent an apartment, Sandy went apartment hunting with us and soon we were living together.

Easter week we were all heading for home. Sandy announced that she was going to stay at our apartment because her family was busy and wouldn't be home for the holiday. Besides, she said, it was a long trip home and she just couldn't afford it. I persuaded her to go home with me.

My seventeen-year-old brother and my parents lived in an apartment above the sporting goods store and motel that my parents owned and ran. Things were always busy with their hectic work schedule and with aunts and uncles and cousins running in for a few minutes to visit, but everyone in my family did all they could to make Sandy feel welcome. Easter Sunday the store was closed and we all went to church together, then to my aunt's for dinner. I thought it was the perfect day.

That night, however, I awoke to hear choked sobs coming from the bed next to mine. I climbed out of bed and turned on the light. Sandy had her head buried in a pillow as she tried not to wake my family with her sobbing. I sat next to her and lay my hand gently on her shaking shoulders.

"What's wrong, Sandy?" I whispered.

She sat up in bed and wiped her face as I handed her some Kleenex. "Your family is so different from mine. Your parents never fight, they seem to love each other." She looked at me for a long time, emotion worked its way across her face.

"When my father stops drinking and drags himself out of his chair we know it's time to get out of the house." She began sobbing again, talking only when she could catch her breath. "He begins finding fault with everything he sees, then he starts pounding on people. My mother has been saving money in the cookie jar so she can get a divorce, but she never can get enough. She just keeps having more babies."

I held Sandy tight and ached with the pain that moved from her shoulders into my own heart. My safe little world had protected me from this kind of agony, and in 1968 people did not talk about their problems as openly as they do today. I had no idea how to help my friend except to be there whenever she needed to talk.

The next fall the social unrest that had been affecting the rest of our nation finally reached northern Minnesota. We participated in peace marches protesting the Viet Nam war, we worked for civil rights, and we knew without a doubt that our generation would change the world. Sandy loved all this, and she listened carefully to the talk of new drugs that could make you happy and free your thoughts. We argued about these drugs as we sat in the coffee houses late at night, but they were light arguments. I was certain that Sandy would never do anything so risky.

Then one odious morning everything changed. The front page of the newspaper carried the story of a young boy who had taken his father's hunting rifle and killed him because he could no longer tolerate his father's abuse. Sandy got the terrible news from the paper. No one had bothered to find her and hold her as she received the mind deranging news of what had happened in her own family.

Sandy refused to let me accompany her to the funeral and came back changed. Soon we were arguing intensely about her use of marijuana and to stop our arguments she left our apartment and moved in with her boyfriend. Next, she was using LSD. I spent the longest night of my life following Sandy up and down the railroad tracks that ran alongside Lake Superior, trying to save Sandy from herself as she endured a terrible reaction caused by her drug. We were in my favorite place, but that black night the medley of waves did nothing to calm me.

By that time I was doing my student teaching. I would soon be leaving college and Minnesota because I had already accepted a teaching job in Wisconsin. I frantically wanted to help my friend but had no idea what to do. My faith in God remained strong, but my prayers seemed to enter an empty universe and brought no answers. I confided in my student teaching supervisor who advised me to say nothing. He convinced me that rather than receiving help Sandy would go to jail for her drug use.

Soon it was graduation day and I moved far from my college town. Life sped by. I married and had three children. I wrote to Sandy regularly, she never wrote back, but I visited her whenever I could. When my third child, a son, was born Sandy gave birth to a daughter. Sandy's sister adopted little Kathy because Sandy wasn't capable of taking care of her baby. Sandy continued in a downward spiral passing from one social service agency to another.

Sandy stayed in my heart and my prayers. I was haunted by the fact that someone should have known how to help her. I earned a masters degree in working with the emotionally disturbed, I wanted to help teenagers before they became unreachable.

Our family moved back to my college town. We added a fourth child to our home, a four-year-old girl who had been removed from her abusive home and made available for adoption. As the years passed, Sandy no longer knew who I was. She became a bag lady spending her nights at the shelter. When I stopped to talk to her on the street, she answered my questions pleasantly but there was no recognition in her eyes. When I told her my name she looked at me blankly. My love for Sandy had changed the course of my life, yet I couldn't tell her.

When my third child was sixteen I was teaching English to young people just his age. By now I had established a reputation for working well with emotionally needy students and the school counselors made sure that many of these needy made it into my class. On the first day of the new semester a girl entered my class with sharp blue eyes in a freckle filled face. When I heard her laughter my heart stopped as I was swept into the past. She introduced herself, her name was Kathy.

Kathy eventually told me her story which gave me the opportunity to explain that her birth mother and I had been friends. I always throw myself into my teaching with a passion and I work hard to give all my students the special help they need, but when it came to Kathy I had to wage battle within. For once in my life I wanted to create a teacher's pet.

On a pungent spring day that brought the smell of lilacs into the classroom, I leaned against the window sill and explained the details of literary analysis to the students in Kathy's class. As I talked, I absently gazed out the window thinking only of the material I was working so hard to explain. My voice froze. Sandy was trudging up the steep hill only one story beneath my classroom, dragging her bag along the rough surface of the sidewalk. For no reason that I could discern she stopped, turned, raised her still blue eyes up to mine, and held up her hand as though in greeting. She couldn't have recognized me, yet it felt like a benediction.

BIOGRAPHIES

Arlene Atwater is an abstract painter and writer. She received a mentorship with short story writer and novelist Amy Bloom through the Loft Literary Center's 2001-2002 Mentor Series and recently won honorable mention in the Marguerite duPont Boden short story competition sponsored by the Nation League of American PEN Women. She works at the University of Minnesota Duluth.

Anthony Bukoski's stories have appeared in Poland, Canada, and the United States in such journals as *Quarterly West, Arcana, New Letters,* and *The Literary Review.* Southern Methodist University Press published his short story collections *Children of Strangers* (1993) and *Polonaise* (1999).

Jan Chronister lives on 38 acres in Maple, Wisconsin and spends her time writing, reading, gardening and designing costumes for the Duluth Playhouse.

Eric Gadzinski teaches English at Lake Superior State University. A number of his poems have appeared in various small publications. He is currently collaborating with his wife, Anishinaabe artist Carolyn Dale, on a chapbook of poems and illustrations: *Four Directions.*

Karin Jacobson teaches English and composition at the University of Minnesota Duluth (UMD). When she's not teaching, Karin pursues her other passions: rock climbing, running and mountain biking. Currently on a sabbatical from UMD, she and Evan are climbing in Joshua Tree and Yosemite, and living in their 1992 Chevy conversion van.

Patricia Kirkpatrick has been awarded poetry fellowships from the National Endowment for the Arts, the Bush Foundation, the Minnesota State Arts Board, and the Loft. Her poems have been published in many magazines and anthologies, including *The Threepenny Review* and *Antioch Review.* She teaches literature and writing at Hamline University and is interested in connecting poetry with new audiences. She lives in Saint Paul with her family.

Kate Kysar's book of poetry *Dark Lake* will be released by Loonfeather Press in February. Kysar's poems have appeared in several literary magazines including *Painted Bride Quarterly, Permafrost, Communitas, Dust and Fire, The Midland Review, The Talking Stick,* and *The Minnesota Poetry Calendar.* She was a finalist for the SASE/Jerome fellowship in 2001. She teaches English at Anoka-Ramsey Community College in Minneapolis, lives with her family in St. Paul, and often vacations on the north shore of Lake Superior.

After graduate school, **Lynn Maria Laitala** returned to her family home in Winton, Minnesota, where she recorded oral histories for the Minnesota Historical Society. That work inspired her to write historical fiction. Her story "Child of the Place" won recognition in the 1999 Lake Superior Writers' Contest. Her first novel, *Down from Basswood,* was published in December. Lynn lives in Bennett, Wisconsin, where she is working on a second novel.

Diane Sher Lutovich was born and raised in Hibbing and graduated from the University of Minnesota. Since moving to California she has been a writer, a business consultant, mother, and, most recently, grandmother. She is currently executive vice-president of California Poets in the Schools. A long-time writer of poetry, she has been published in *Lucid Stone, Barnabee Mountain,* and *Sonoma Mandala,* among others. She is also the author of *Nobody's Child: How Older Women Say Good-Bye to their Mothers,* published recently by Baywood Publishers.

Mark Maire has spent most of his adult life in Duluth, having then earned an M.A. in library science from the University of Iowa, and working as a reference librarian and cataloger ever since. His poetry has appeared in a number of literary magazines, including the *Arizona Quarterly, Birmingham Poetry Review, Descant, Farmer's Market, New Laurel Review,* and *Wolf Head Quarterly.*

Lisa McKhann, Duluth, has an M.A. in creative writing and teaches ocassional workshops at the Loft about what writers can borrow from other art forms. She's currently exploring using poetry with modern dance and visual art.

Margi Preus writes plays, stories, articles, opera libretti, children's books and grocery lists. She is a sometime teacher and an all-the-time mom. Up until a few minutes ago, she directed Colder by the Lake Comedy Theater.

Mary Kay Rummel's new collection of poems, *Green Journey, Red Bird*, was published in September, 2001 by Loonfeather Press. Her poetry book, *This Body She's Entered*, was published by New Rivers Press as a Minnesota Voices Award winner and a poetry chapbook, *The Long Road Into North*, was published by Juniper Press. Her poems have appeared in *Nimrod*, and in the anthology, *33 Minnesota Poets, Bloomsbury Review, Luna* and *Water-Stone*. She is a professor at the University of Minnesota Duluth and lives in Fridley.

Yvonne Rutford is currently completing her MFA in Writing at Goddard College in Vermont. She lives along a North Shore river in rural Duluth, Minnesota, and draws most of her creative inspiration from the natural world around her. When she's not writing creative prose and poetry, she offers freelance technical writing services regionally, and teaches writing courses at Wisconsin Indianhead Technical College in Superior, Wisconsin.

Jason Splichal teaches English and Speech Communications at Eau Claire South and is the author of two books of poetry: *The Complications of Contact* and *Flashbulb Sun Eggshell Moon*. He is the co-editor of the poetry journal *Fuse*, and his work has appeared in *NOTA, The International Library of Poetry*, and *The Free Radical*.

Amy Jo Swing has lived in Alaska, Indiana, Texas, and Minnesota. She has a B.A. in English from Purdue University and an M.F.A. in poetry from Southwest Texas State University. She first came to Duluth, Minnesota in 1992, and owns a home on Observation Hill with her partner and their two border collies. She teaches English at Lake Superior College.

For a passel of years, **Caitlin Taylor** has been doing and thinking, figuring and noticing, wondering and hoping and hanging' on. She's been loving and fuming, laughing and crying, struggling and relishing. And now, from a perch in Duluth, she's writing it down.

Colin Keith Thomsen is a student, writer, media activist, adventurer and expatriate Duluthian currently stationed in Minneapolis. His work has appeared in several obscure leftist publications such as the *Pulse of the Twin Cities, The Free Press*, and *Clamor* magazine. Colin currently is the proud holder of both an Industrial Workers of the World union card and a Minnesota Class D Driver's License.

Susan Niemela Vollmer was born and raised in Ely, Minnesota and lived near Duluth for 17 years before moving to Rice Lake, Wisconsin, where she currently lives with her husband and daughters. She teaches in the gifted/talented program in the Rice Lake elementary schools. Her work has been published in *Minnesota Monthly, North Coast Review, North Country Journal, Dust and Fire, Women's Stories Must Be Told, The Finnish American Reporter, New World Finn, Minnesota Poetry Calendar,* and other publications.

Lou Killian Zywicki began to work at writing seriously three years ago, when she began taking her summers off from teaching to write. Since then, she has sold more than 20 essays, memoirs, and short stories to national magazines and anthologies. She is in the process of writing a young adult novel and is working at marketing a children's picture book. In addition, she teaches literature, writing, and communications at the Secondary Technical Center in Duluth, is the mother of four grown children, and lives with her husband, Ernie, in a nature paradise south of Carlton, MN.